MW00333898

IN THE LAURELS, CAUGHT

BY THE SAME AUTHOR

Polyverse (Sun & Moon Press)
The Sleep That Changed Everything (Wesleyan University Press)
Bagatelles for Cornell (Propolis Press)

IN THE LAURELS, CAUGHT

(NC-ode)

LEE ANN BROWN

FENCE MODERN POETS SERIES

FENCE
BOOKS

ALBANY, NEW YORK

©Lee Ann Brown 2013
All rights reserved

COVER IMAGE
Double Bow Knot pattern and draw-down by Frances Louisa
Goodrich. Used with permission of the Southern Highland Craft
Guild Archives.

Cover design and illustration by Noah Saterstrom
Book design by Rebecca Wolff

Published in the United States by Fence Books, Science Library,
320 University at Albany, 1400 Washington Avenue, Albany,
NY 12222

WWW.FENCEPORTAL.ORG

Fence Books are printed in Canada by The Prolific Group and
distributed by Small Press Distribution and Consortium Book
Sales and Distribution.

Library of Congress Cataloguing in Publication Data
Brown, Lee Ann [1963-]
In the Laurels, Caught/Lee Ann Brown

Library of Congress Control Number: 2013932324

ISBN 13: 978-1-934200-67-4

FIRST EDITION
10 9 8 7 6 5 4 3 2

Fence Books are published in partnership with the University at
Albany and the New York State Writers Institute, and with help
from the New York State Council on the Arts and the National
Endowment for the Arts.

FOR JONATHAN WILLIAMS

CONTENTS

River Codex

You can't go home again
But you can come here.
　　—DAVE BRINKS, THE SCHOOL OF THE IMAGINATION

Just because a cat has her kittens in an oven,
You don't call them biscuits.
　　　　　—VICKI LANE, *Art's Blood*

These traditions are not good because they are old. It's the
other way around.
　　　　　—RICHARD CHASE

The national security blanket is a crazy quilt.
　　　　　— ELIZABETH WILLIS

All people are your people.
　　　　　— JAMES BALDWIN, *Another Country*

burning for folklore
　　　　　— ROD SMITH

I

SOME BOOKS OF DAYS

so was the world
      when the French Broad River was young

in which it now finds itself

older than the mountains

DAYLILY

A Daylily's blossom
only lasts one day

Binnorie O Binnorie

My grandmother showed me
how to have my say

the glory O the glory

Now every time I see a faded drooping bud

Binnorie O Binnorie

I deadhead it like she did
so the rest can live on

The story O the story

only the Nile and ironically the New River predate

I wake up to a wall of moths

so old as to be   practically devoid of fossils

I want an Oulipian quilted talk

POLLEN PATH

Lightning to clear us

    What stars

beauty springs

    For & after

    the "Bee In"

I reached it:

               Beauty above me

      Beauty to the left of me   *Beauty to the right of me*

               Beauty below me

    Means that I am *inside* the flower

        a Bee
      on the [pollen] path

that finds
that fine gold powder

I have seen
on two separate occasions, both deaths

held by the french

                    I want a Stitch-n-Bitch

It's their house too,
　　　　those wasps
Major nesting instruments here

I'm 40.853 years old
　　　　& this is my first house
　　　　on the first night

of Diana's Day
　　　　it's a Friday &

the newest moon waxes
and astounds the water calendar

　Front door faces East and uphill
　Porch faces South to the side
　Deck faces West across the river
　The fireplace side faces North

At the heart of the house is a spiral
Awake at 3:15
Inspect our home to be
Arrange the furniture in my mind
Hope I don't clutter it up too much

The startling thing is the green roof
You see upon approach
Round the top of the hill and Bam

There it is
above the Laurel Hells

flamethrowing into french territory

　　　　　　　　I want a Poem

The First oldest river in the world is the Nile
the Second is the New
and the Third is this French Broad River

Early in the spring
        blooms the Mountain Laurel
locally called Ivy

Also coves of rhododendron,
        locally called Laurel

Laurel Hells: Kept 'em out as well as in

        said Kephart

Just past midsummer,
        black raspberries
                and wineberries
all in a tangle of foreign invasives

    Joe Pye Weed Corridor has established itself
    along alternative names for our road

                Bumpety-Bump-Bump
                Mullen Way
                        (already knew people boiled it for
                        Vitamin C, but just learned from
                        19-year-old in St. Paul, Virginia
                        that the huge soft leaves were used
                        by pioneers as baby diapers and
                        toilet paper—that beats the Sears
                        Catalogue any day)

*the shape of the Appalachian Trail
        complete with mileposts*

Maidenhair Lane
Pokeberry Drive
French Broad Overlook
Winding Stair
Ferny Corridor
Valley of Norway
Wineberry Chute
Over the Lindens
Little Bear Road
Goldilocks Turnpike Extension

I named our house Reality House
as opposed to Dream House

because I need to be grounded
on this mountain

also after my daughter's
hidden middle name

Dirt Daubers attempt to spit out a nest
on the Japanese screen

in this temperate rain forest
working its mysterious ways

French Broad River

flows northwest
gets joined by

Time stands still here
    And the river does not move

Pigeon Little Pigeon

    as in Pigeon Forge
      as in Dollywood

"the dollywood of my neon heart's overflow"

A LETTER OUT

So it's one of my first days writing here. I take off to the old turnpike and stop in at the Ramsey cemetery. It reminds me of the one Linda took me to with a view of the Flatirons where we searched for the unmarked grave of Edward Steele and instead found a heart-shaped rock. A blue and grey vista of ridges fold around my home. These mountains are *old* mountains. Rockies: 5 million years old, Appalachians: 500 million. This is a windblown hilltop cemetery, which are plentiful here, like an overgrown version of some family's private one. Graves from the 1800s, some with lambs. I am drawn to a newer black stone with an RV carved into it, careening from bumpy road to straight path. A bumpy road to heaven leaving a rough existence for a straight-arrow afterlife? I would like to be buried way out in the country so I wouldn't take up too much room—here if they'd let me. There's a gray granite headstone down on the bypass where someone wrecked, but unlike roadside memorials made of flowers and small styrofoam crosses, it gives the impression she is buried right there. The white angel in front of the RV stone has fallen over and so have the yellow plastic flowers. I debate whether to climb up the hill to right them, but head down to town instead.

A man walks into Zuma, so familiar. Almost like the jolt of seeing an old lover—some electric surprise. Then I realize he's an old friend from college I haven't seen for twenty some years. The connection springs up in an unexpected

Nolichucky

White Gap

to the flatlands of Tennessee

place—turns out he's FROM here, moved back home seven years ago, teaches philosophy in East Tennessee. His eyes light up that same way. So THAT's why I liked his soft lilt so much way back then. I struggle with the anti-essentialists who say we cannot identify Appalachia—but yes we are all strange coincidental processes in time and space that somehow (strange attractors) are brought into each others' orbits yet again.

This is what I was writing before Keith walked in (eavesdropping as I am wont to do):

It's funny—it's like circle after circle up here. He had a new kick drum. He put it in an old plastic bag and blew smoke into it until the drum skin matched the old ones. When you play a club, by the end of the night your sense of smell has totally checked out.

An approximation of the above was spoken by this guy who I assumed was a Marshall regular (trying to learn the new human territory). I thought I would get to listen to him again but I never have so far. He had this amazing blonde trailing Mohawk down his bare back, talking to a child support payment worker. The courthouse lawyer bites his chicken wrap. A little baby flies in, buoyed up by his or her daddy in hunting fatigues. Two young women behind the counter with brown ponytails and very different stories.

its Confluence
with the Holston River
makes the Tennessee One

down by the banks of the O—hio

I want to meet you people but I am only on the first level time-wise. Even though it's my home state, I'm way out in the country now. There's something in this impulse that wants me to write it with light.

finally the Mississippi
flows to

"...WEED!"

— Lorine Niedecker

1. It's only fun because you are pulling some up to let some others thrive.

2. Always grasp low on the stem to get the most roots you can.

3. Whack the root clump on the ground and shake off the good dirt

   (Variation: Root ball javelin).

4. Make sure you're not pulling up the lilies.

5. or the mint

6. or hearty begonias

7. or pokeberries even.

8. Vary the speed

9. Work methodically as one variation.

   (Ditto for heights and varieties
   of what you delete)

10. Notice varying qualities of each,
    sporadic bird calls.

*the Gulf of Mexico
must be where the mermaids come from*

11. Don't go barefoot like me.

12. Mantis, bumblebee.

13. Pull big ones and forge new ground.

14. Go back and pull the
                little ones
            that have grown up

                    as your back was
                        turned

15. Wonder about the evolution of farm implements.

16. Observe what plants grow in relation to
one another:
        tiny forest, oasis, ecosystem, terrarium...

17. See another grasshopper.

18. Think about woman in the paper who got
rid of her
        weeds by flattening the hillside with boxes
and doing
        snow angels on top of them.

19. Forget what you were thinking.

Brett Evans writes   *"French Broad:*
                    Here in New Orleans thats two separate things."

ANSWERING MACHINE

1.

This is JOHN DAvis

I just called you to see
if you was OK up on the mountain

I hear you had some, uh
                    "Litt'l company"

Fuzzy neighbors In your house

That sounds like the little girl
                    that . . .
(Ruby's voice in background)
Yes, Little Goldilocks

So I guess we'll have to name you *Goldilocks*

That the Three Bears
          Come to see

Y'all have a good evening
We'll be talking to you

          Bye Bye

                                        water
              too thick to drink, too thin to plow

2.

Hey

this is Louise—
down at the foot of the hill
Thanks for calling
John about the Bear
Give me a call when you get a chance

Thanks Hon—
Have a good day
and
You watch that baby, Honey

He's hungry. . . . He's hungry

excess
the mills spinning
down the hill

RURAL SURREAL

lorine niedecker

wanted to get away from the anecdotal
into an arc of sound

vertical

cicada skins
we'd wear as pins

circadian skins
we'd swear as kin

geological
mycelleum   *over*

PONDER AUTO

Ponder took out his little razor
to scrape off my old inspection sticker

Then he started pasting on the new one
That'll be nine dollars and ten cents.

Well I hope it passes
says my Dad, Little Dagwood sweat marks
coming out of his head

Ponder's reply:
Well, ye wanted it to didn't ye?

Double Bow Knot is also a dance

FOAMHENGE

for Jonathan Williams

Upon coming across M. Cline's "Foamhenge"
near Natural Bridge, Virginia in much the same
manner as when driving across England from
London to Glastonbury we "accidently" came
across Stonehenge. The plaque says it all.

THANK YOU FOR VISITING FOAMHENGE, A FULL
SCALE REPLICA of the mystical Stonehenge OF ENGLAND.

PLEASE ENJOY YOURSELF AT THIS SITE, BUT PLEASE
BE GENTLE. IT IS FOAM NOT STONE . . . **Built in six
weeks by 4–5 mexicans + 1 crazy white man**

TWO GREAT reasons <u>YOU WILL NOT DEFACE</u> MY
SCULPTURE

> 1) It's a federal offense to deface public OR
> private property ⓦ a possible 1 YEAR IN
> PRISON + $10,000 fine.

> 2) SOMETIMES I HIDE + WATCH. I'LL LET
> YOU SCRATCH ON FOAMHENGE AS I DO
> THE SAME TO YOUR PARKED VEHICLE.
> DON'T BE SURPRISED, I'M NUTS ENOUGH
> TO DO IT!
>
> M.CLINE

Dont raise the hand until it's time
to go underneath

BLACK IS THE COLOR

Yellow is the color of my true love's crossbow
Yellow like the color of the sun

Black is the color of a strangled rainbow
Exactly the color of my love

— Elvis Perkins

Black is the color of my true love's Arrows
Black is the color of the cat
Black is the color of the nighttime mountains
Black is the color of the heavy stuff

Black is the color of
              the ribbon snake
        hanging over the
              lip of the face jug

Black is the color of outside my
window

Inky lumen in
   gray silkier modes

Black is the pattern on
the woven snake's back
  pitch eye light
slides coolly
  into night's ear

or
it's really messing with them

Inky muffled trees

   shadow bloom
  punctuated by
   silver light

Blue black bear paw
Exactly the color of my blood

Black iris of my eye
widening at night

& while he's going through those little doors

DOUBLE SOUTHERN REGISTER

Here in the Appalachians

the phrase

I don't care

gives consent

Form follows function

Form mirrors function

The Mace family chair is said to

make the sitter quote

Forget about chairs

Meaning

Chairs are ruined for you

Once you've sat in one you can sit in no other

(up North it's *Fuhgeddaboudit*)

the end lady counter clockwise round the outside

After tasting tomatoes picked

fresh from a hot garden

I once wrote:

Tomatoes like warm bleeding hearts

and could eat no other after that—

ghostlike grocery store "hothouse" varietals

did nothing for me

But songs are made from a rarified material

Language gives them a different nature

An antique that cannot be

contained, stroked or sold

A coverlet that will not rot

nor unravel

swing yr panther   she'll swing you

IT REACHES OUT TO GRAB YOU

(lines to be read in any order)

It reaches out to grab you

on the Brink of Spring

watch out for red vines

fresh as Indian Pipe

Pipsissiwa is my favorite

Filtered the lines

Along the creekbed

All connected underground

Plant in the whole entire world

Jump start you are

The golden morning breaks

*Sometimes Lee Ann rhymes
and sometimes she don't*

Out to the right
Don't take all night

tie 'em up
      lady lead around

II
MICROKOSMOS

branch
neighbors —

the ones on
your
same winding
road

I move
between
town &
mountain

context to
be
open

freeing

ON ORGANIC FORM

It's the tree's choice
what the treehouse looks like
in the end

Codex
to the rejection of
    southern closure
a river

made of
many streams
both named
& unnamed

O Mushroom please don't
mind if a toad sits on you
Every rainy night

spill into
the
gulf

What
have we
done
to its
living waters

sing them
backwards
to the
source

Little by little
My sweater dresses
turn into shirts

in a
different
        order

    how they
        come

        but form
    this time

                they
                evolve
            (the poems)

MOONFLOWER

dies with first frost

but

til then

written across —

OUTRAGEOUS BEHAVIOR

Just sitting there
Doing nary a thing

like a

weave

could be
combed through
later

RACECAR IS A PALINDROME

The car of tomorrow
has yet to be driven

Wilma
Dykeman
saturation
job

editors almost took out

THE ONLY JOKE I CAN REMEMBER

Why does the Madonna always look so sad
in paintings?

She was hoping for a girl.

her chapter on
pollution
    the first
      ecological writing

    seven years before Silent Spring

      history
        geology
        trials
         & stories
          Structure
          of rime
         16 then
           20

PORCH ADVICE

You've written the poem—
Hell, might as well write the book!

Just add some of them Roman Numerals

all the
potentialities
within

local
history
specificity

each of ours
spread out
a firmament
of the everyday
weave

OVERHEARD AT BALLAD LECTURE

Well, it's *not* dining table music

(How do I
stop)

from
singing

LITTLE BLACK BOXES

When asked
could she read music

Quick as a snake
answered

Not enough to hurt my singing

How can
    I keep

   so they wont
      unravel

          Close off
       the threads and the seams

SHEILA KAY ON THE CHILD BALLADS

When I went away to college
somebody asked me if I knew any Child ballads.

Yes, I answered,
I learned them as a Child.

over a
burning island

live
streamed

on a pyre
in golden
cap

ON WORKING FROM HISTORY

Cultures are ribbons
You can get ahold of

I Best   do that

is a
        taxonomy

Well the poems grow more divergently

WIND

Willows drape down
In the water
Near the blown
Down barn

like seeing
a particular
bird or
star

It's a SIGN

Venus   Jupiter   Mars   & were
                            intermittent

                        the planets
                            conjunct in
                                    Codex

OPEN
EGGS

pro
 wrestling
  the same

Nascar
 evolved
  round the
   bend

ANGEL FOOD
SUSPENDED

two Tanks —
one for gas
one for lightning —

PONDER
AUTO

moon
shine & goat milk
instead of
just wine & milk

grits
instead
of
what

Handmade
in America

X-PLODING
TARGETS

objects

rooms
food

45

LOTS OF CANDY   JOHN   3:16

mythic & real

A Barthes
Mythology
   of the South — abstracted

or what about

FRESH PRODUCE
A   HEAD

the
everyday
framed
explained

a
catalogue of
daily objects
beautiful useful

a tender
buttons
of
the
southern

WHAT A BURGER

WHAT A   URGE

are pools
    poetry or
        are pools
        prose

                    through letters
            back   forth

                                words in
                    country
                        music
                    illuminated

MADISON

MAD SON

the river's
Form I
imagined

pools
streams
between

one
poem,
one
prose
alternative

a lake
  with
real painted
    waves   is in actuality
                                only a view of a
                        continually
                                flowing river

                                      When I
                            first wanted the
                                form of this
                                    book to know
                            only a view of a
                        continually
                                flowing river

through Asheville
then to Lousiana
& then to the
ocean

III
MIDSUMMER CUSHION

velvety peaks of the old America, the mound America.

—PETER CULLEY

City & Milky Way
Still rule the day
The way the roses
Ride the vine
Look for us there

We live out of time

—COBY BATTY

Just another diamond day
Just a blade of grass

—VASHTI BUNYAN

the river
runs up from
Transylvania

then
here
specifically

we can see
it from the
porch
a pool

even animals
plants

MOSS PILLOW

Visiting Peter on some planisphere where all the emails go when erased, where the servers overflow. To stand in a high-up place on all the mounds of England, at a great height on Glastonbury Tor, we have not to fall but to lift off straight arrows. We are already half way there. Level seven. Dust from all dead flower petals, scattered ash. Ashgrove is painted, and now the yellow flame room, also the Hymning Room. Our rooms are naming themselves one by one. The house is meant to serve us, not we the house. Bed us, encase us, no other way around us. They live in Mars Hill. So where's Venus? Green tendrils grow around new nerves. Tiny orange spiders are born from eggs. A fly just landed on Conrad's stanza and showed it to me anew: "it is / just / so."

& who before
them?

who

we can
still speak
with

immersion
for a season

DEAR OTHER MIRANDA

The grass repeats after her, writing a letter of spirals and eyeballs. Opal Whitely in the making leaves sleep without it breaking. Plaster cave-in the day before arrival. Sweetheart Rose knows her colors as webs catch white dew. New steps "float" over the old dangerous stone. Tatting the source of all language into a hair wreath woven from all who visit here. A guest book might be easier but I wrote a poem there when I heard that Robert died. Old Rugged Crosses in the trails above the house. "Poke Sallit" is cooked spring greens for today's nuptials. We ate those pancakes and a few tips of evergreens for a tart snack to keep us going on the rock hop. A black cat enters under the plastic Jack O'Lantern filled with crayons. It's spring. We hadn't missed the cherry blossoms of 22nd Street, but flung them in the air with Giovanni, Penelope and Gwendolyn at Seal Park.

the
Cherokee
kingdom   school
                                farther
                                    west

                                            they were
                                                    on this
                                            island
                                        of course

DOUSING FOR DUMMIES

Blockade is pink lemonade made from strawberry library books. The Totoro house hums a deep song in yonder glen. You're a fragment of my imagination. Experience wafts its checkered travelers in with a thumbprint. Vexed, then fixed. Seeing signs shaped like huge shoes. Fox Church Road sprang up on our left. Bright blue-green beetle vale under a rock, Keats' favorite letter was V. She spins it like a tiny DJ on her alphabet box. Windy Mandy over the wall straggles in with beeping shoes, lit up like a kite. The leaves are out of pollen or soon will be. Who are you calling a verdant lush. Here, mommy hold this mess. Don't say to me. I don't like to. Blap is my friend. He's a boy. He's a ghost who lives in New York. He painted with me. His hair is yellow. He painted pink hair. His hair is red. I *am* Blap. Here are some "piecle puzzles" for you. I will make some more for you. Are you a Cat Bus? We're getting married. I'm marrying this tree. Cheeky Dickie married a Chickadee. You're dead chuffed with yourself. Scraping away at a bleeding book. And you should be too. So where's my werewolf pillow?

some kind of
sacred
geometry

people come
here for dreams

carve out
their
realities

TOMORROW LIBRARY

This kaleidoscope makes all reality look like Queen Anne's Lace. The apogee of a circle slows and balances only once or twice a summer. Just now it did. Being a mother is like picking up the six grains of dried brown rice off the floor and getting out the Whack-a-Mole when you "should be . . ." Mindful puppets or otherwise trying to click two words together like rocks. Too many "should ofs" make me a sick pup. Fly up the stairs to see the Virginia Woolf doll in a compromising position. It could be a cat. So many black and white butterflies out whipping poor Will. Oscillation of the idyllic, writing in someone else's book. Slumping and cracking nuts. Sleepy caterpillar before cocoon phaseout, or is it dead? Maypops turn to July fireflowers. Midsummer cushions over ripe rhododendron. The black raspberries finally ripen. Do I trust this new kind of union? Folded and flipped. The shapes she drew on me are still there. Hanabi or 'Fire Flowers' on my leg.

the
    architect
who said

        that
    the ending is
            only the
                beginning where

                        you get
                new
                    ideas

BATHING SUIT BANTER

How the box turtle leverages or jacks up her front when closing her shell. The rain's up in the road a couple places, also found dangling from pine needles. Santa Claus is growing beans at the bottom of Bumpedty-Bump Bump. They built this different since I been here. Blowing through a widow of opportunity. The moths converge on my spot at night, the only light. Human genome desire, mapping out conscious ellision. Let's trap her to keep her safe. I'm hanging, I'm falling said the girl said the girl. I want to nurse said the turtle said the girl. Dot – Dot – Dash – Nurse – Dot – Dash - Dot –Dash —— Bat O Up Foot Up Oh. Firefly transmission. Upon blowing bubbles: "What comes after I?" "Is it J?" "No! I Got It!" And that ball looks like a BIG BIG BIG BIG BIG BIG P!

the
matrix of
names

Spillcorn   *Pattern*

Stackhouse
Patton

SCRATCH FACTOR

Jack all impish enough for my mothercrush's youth. O nether astounding lads, you get the spanking machine. Silver white dragon tigers racoon-teer their fears, lie down on the African king bed. A thrush in the throat, the musical shuttle. The Girl of Limberlost all moldy in a box. Pink plastic elephants, poisonous water snakes. Errands karaoked me. Mesmerizing irises dilate a solid body. The whole family lives in a box of light.

each room made from

a different wood

built

along the

river

HEY!

Let's make a chicken out of a hand
says the flat champagne.
Centuries ago, the same thing was said
and now it's Thursday because they roll.
Oh. Hi, Little Angel,
Will you fly for Baby Jesus?
I will, I will, said the Fly.
How do bugs deconstruct so quickly?
Maybe, there's a handprint in the hand part.
Hey guys, what happened?

cuts across

it   *& over*

the tables   mountains of
rock   too shallow
for barges

BOO!

You're tickling my poem
You don't sing through it —
You put it *behind* music.
In this era which begets
Such inventions as the echinechea lollipop
in between the washer and the delicate dryer,
I hand off the candle tangerine.
Unstopped by daily business we
transition successfully into ecstacy
by way of you, my mountain dewer.

*from
southeast
to northwest*

*the way
the year itself
suggests
a form*

*the moon
each
multiple
name*

DECODER RING

Hey, keep going my love says
ten lines can hold the music
we screwed onto the wall
I fluctuate between nothing
and
too much work, worry, success
proves to hitch us up to a meteor
over Jupiter or at least to Keith Green's
Forks of Ivy while the great connector
insulator bids on the angel seen in this
subterfuge fadeout wakeup walkup

pattern
    seen from
        above as
topological

Map

        the way you
    understand it
        backwards

                            the river
                            runs they
                            tell me
                        atypically

THE DYNAMIC FLOORWALKER

In Chapter Three a nest is built outside the varying weather as a low dose of love time release formula. It decides to rest the tablet thus. Perched for to fly through the underbrush into unowned lands downhill through the brown leaves whose voices would surely whisper of vexed attempts to groan or grow rogue ginseng. Roan attachments to open raccoons stopgap that creek. Not tongue in cheek, though something's injured. I put back that decapitated head of last night's dream doll-like boy and send him out into the world of his own accord.

*but leads
to stories
which can
be rearranged*

*block of
a pattern*

or rewoven into

FOCUS

Our commune is fulminating. I hear a distant meow in the music. A percolating freebie knows no bounds. I correspond across the time space focus forecast. Through the forest on the way to gown town, I access the turnpike's subconscious. Getting chillier with the wind on the goats near where I was trapped by the trees still wild up here. My hair. Tom's favorite skyscraper's window voiture. Mondrian on a good day clocking coffee because focus I cannot despite the sequins of events.

who does that help
how far does that go   if I find out

their names

the taxonomy
is just a
way to begin

BUT I DIDN'T GET THE IMAGE

It's of a winter tree with brown leaves
that are still there and flutter wildly in a pattern
and I always wondered, do those hanger-ons
get pushed out when the new ones come in spring?
We listen to the freezing stream at the bottom
of the hill run safely off the mountain.
Let's go see the way up to the bee tree
and scoop out actual honey like a bear named Moonbeam
who can actually lucidly dream.
Once you were a bear and I could have you.
Now you're a man and I can't have you
Which would you choose, man by day, bear by night
or the other way around but with amnesia?

left up for years   rumors of
                   overt graffiti
                   on official road signs

                          sign on back
                     of pick up truck
                     immigration law
                     commentary

BROWN'S DREAM

Just now there were these women or people telling me about the habits of bees to be collected. They were amassing around some flower and you must let them go afterwards to find their Hive or Queen. We are on the very mountaintop and I am afraid that they are too far from the Queen to reunite. They're in a cup or stocking with their stingers sticking through the mesh. They must be released, the sooner the better, or their powers will amass to sting, breaking out of the container. What does this have to do with the new kitten who wants affection so strongly she breaks down the doors to get to us? I woke with the phrase "a habit like kissing" or was it "a habit such as kissing" which turned into "the kissing custom." What does this have to do with the yellow jacket nest I asked Michael Redfox to destroy tomorrow or the artwork of the Beehive Collective I just received in PO Box 13? What is the form of writing down a dream? Should this dream be in line breaks? I must say it was extraordinary finding Alyssa talking about eating apples and honey and the different ways sweetness comes into them before our drive home and the poet as ecstatic. I said that poetry could go anywhere, do anything, even practice law. She then said, "I am glad that is your mission." Dreams continue into the day. Seeing that miniature owl on the way home flash its round golden eyes up at us from the road (good thing I was going slow) and then it flying and landing on a branch almost made up for the horrible thing that happened to the box turtle whose shell could not protect her from the wheel of a car on the road before me. I'm sorry to report that turtle meat is red.

like an Obama
supervillain cardboard cutout
at the Ingles exit

about the one African
American family
lived in town
years ago

might as well
    tell the
        story   *this is one place*
                            race is mentioned

                                    in the book

IV
FIELDWORK

Springs further up

with names
like
Freedom   not only

                  the spirit
                     of
                  community   Converging
                                          streams

FREE ADMISSION TO OUR SALE

Wood Martin Houses
Drywall Lift
All Terrain Tricycle
NASCAR Calculator
13 PC. Screwdriver Set
Sliding Door Curio (Subject to Availability!)
Arc Welder
Plasma Cutter
Superfly Monkey
Recoiling Air Hose
Deluxe Kneepads
5 PC. Brass Quick Coupler Set---
Camouflage Jacket
Inflatable Bounce Castle
4 PC. Cat or Dog Plant Stake Set
Resin Snail Set
24" Resin Potato Sack Race Girl
Poly Bird Bath
6 PC Sign Maker's Set
1 Ton Wagon (4 wheel dump kit)
Underwater Camera
Inline Tester
25' Tape Measure w/ Hi-Vis Case

4 Days Only!
We've Gone Mad!

*3 churches
converge at Ivy River*

*not planned
that's just where
you go*

*hot
Sundays
3 denominations*

TO RAISE AN A

learning the angle

of the bevel edge

over and over

chisel and hammer

letters are made of

Strokes

Triangles

and

Curves

(Caves)

I

is the first

exercise

in a stone sampler

at its base —

DOME POEM

Dodecahedrons
are the basis for
these pods of wildness
two angular breasts
up on the hillside

Spoleto has one
as you enter town
Bucky Fuller was
there in spirit at
least we walked across

aqueducts—angels
of angles repeat,
repeat and set up
for disaster relief—
Iraq and elsewhere

I saw it on the
Internet—it said
"Geodesic Domes
for Less—Try eBay!"
When I do Google

where
singing meets   *church of the*
biodiverse

on the way
by Sodom
up further

72

I must Stop Shopping
I have enough—more
than enough to keep
me entertained till
The horses come home

To our geodesic dome
On Merrimon they
make "Yomes":
Yurts plus Domes
Equals Yomes but I

Don't know yet if I
Would want one, would you?
wouldn't they mildew? I
like the clear plasti-
cene ones Jimmy O'

by Shelton
White Rock

people came in
to hear
what had been
collected

live

each ridge
grew a white church

like
a white wooden
mushroom

Neal built out near the
the reservoir. One's e-
quipped with night sight
goggles so you can
observe animals

without them smelling
you so much—he made
his sights manifest
and the rest isn't
history—I wonder

about the windex
though being a house
cleaning mom nowadays
It isn't history
because it's still now

ft dead and left for dead
  facedown in the salt

hrough time
  at Allanstand   *the hospital on*
                              the hill collapsing
                                 backwards   *to when it*
                                                    stood new made
                                                    only 150 years
                                                                ago

present but isn't
that history in the
making? (riverside)
extreme home making
art alongside kids

I know how it is
I have this dream where
all Julie Patton's
emails were arranged
in geodesic

patterns and now I
am realizing
that conceptual
strophe as I love
and breathe: Drawn horses.

how it
sounds with
roman numerals
now

& photos
oval frame

to
sew the
coverlet to
the culture

& the "Quare"
Goodrich woman came

DULCIMER

There
is no
"paper
trail"
of
the
Stran
ger
from
the
West
though
a faint
xerox of a
Johnson
City news
clipping tells of
Nineveh Presnell
who "Kills Time" on
"An Unusual Instrument"
"No more beautiful,
soothing music can
be   found" May
Be Similar to
the ones in
the BIBLE
600 Years
before Christ
Nebuchadnezer
King of Babylon
set forth a herald
at what time hear ye
the sound of the cornet
flute harp sackbut psaltry
dulcimer and all kinds of
music ye fall down and
worship Three Feet
Long and made like
a violin they have
3 strings, one
noted by a
stick

pronounced O-my

+

Jean Ritchie told me
to make a big
flappy pick
from a
plastic
coffee
can
lid

my own
branch neighbor

named for
the Biblical

spelled
other than
what

THE
' ISLAND

opens
her Eye in the Night
mid-river looks up at every
one including me, Lee Ann,
of Japan, Charlotte, Manhatta,
Marshall, blessed with a tuneful voice
I am given Poetry in all my Reality
I am given a Tiny Crown to Remind Me
of my Wealth as I Wade in the Water
Sing, beloved world, sing my country song
The Cherokee Syllabary floats fire off the wall
and back into the children's mouths again
Every day, I say to my daughter something
beautiful happens, visits us Now it's some
nightbird's cry 5:15am almost tropical No she
says — three or four beautiful things — tonight
as we pulled up the hill to the house a gigantic
moth the size of a bird danced a while in the
headlights of our paused car then lit aside to perch
on a branch like a bird — what must have been a Fox
streaked through the lights the night before, to bring
me a new name for where I live: Fox Mountain
just like the one I was born to in Japan: Inariyama-koen—
Sing, beloved ones, sing my country ballad
Visitations of Indigo Buntings wrapped in
sun — The Pattern Poems of Syrinx, Axe,
Altar, and Wings all Egg me on to make
this Island. When I say I teach Poetry
Robert Swift Arrow Rose says
You teach people to
speak passionately
and so
I land

Ruby
with him
in the mine

of gathered
folks

lucky to know

MOTH

If I
had taken
that moth with wings exactly like brown leaves
off the sunny window sill yesterday
these bright yellow-green beads of eggs
wouldn't be there today

this house has such irregular doors
no screens are made this size

and I like being preoccupied by all the fluttering

we are visited by the pink and yellow
one dubbed "the Andy Warhol moth"

the moth book says we have found
Anisola rubicunda Fabricius as near as I can tell

The one who looks exactly like two big brown leaves
reappeared last night, kept watch on the lamp
and woke at dawn loudly battling the skylight

If birds are cosmic thoughts,
butterflies, cosmic memories
and bats, cosmic dreams

what are moths?

*purple fox
grapes*

MUSHROOM WALKER

\\\\

our universal veil

is always present

cap and stem unchanging

smell — like marzipan

like the margin

never in fields

absent in locality

is this desire

sticky at first

finally flattened

first mild, then burning

August then October

here and there

some **Deadly**

finally depressed

hung over
      the culvert   *blue*

                                    John in
                                        his field

with a turned up margin

The fruiting body produces

if you let it

our cat-child whelps

agaric

flesh turns red

will we make it

when bruised

I will let you get at my flesh

this time

what you've been salivating after

heavy with cream

sublimate

my urge to please

*these
songs*

*where our
stream sings to
us*

*where we
get the
mail*

some little mushrooms
will get some
more little mushrooms

Clitocybe fragrans
Clitocybe geotropa
Clitocybe gigantea
Clitocybe amethystina
Clitocybe infundibuliformis

the cover

show me

WORDS IN COUNTRY MUSIC

"I wish we could live forever and melt into the sun"
— THE FIVE BLIND BOYS OF ALABAMA

High on a mountain top
The rest of the world just an itty-bitty spot.

My child holds up her hand,
saying it's STOP not SPOT

Ain't coming down no never I'm not
High on a mountain top
High on a mountain top

She walks out on stage at the Biltmore House grounds
in a long white dress just as full
as the moon now coming up over the ridge.

She doubles the moon.

"That was a hard day for music"
says my child

"Notes on Paper Napkins," refers to Harlan's poetic process thusly:

" . . . keeping too much company with a blank sheet of paper,
he heads off to a cocktail lounge for a little eavesdropping."

Or what I like to call "easedropping" because you have to do it eas-
ily, lightly, playfully. There is something playful in southern speech
ways that I love to carry over into song.

mountains
    this ridge
                who live on
                this particular
                            these rocks
                              & rills

Just the other day
a lovely man said
"of an evening"

His nickname for his little girl
was "Scribble-hips"
because of the way she danced.

He said it like this:
"Skribba-hips."

Just last night I got this
Main Street exchange:

That's a beer joint down there

       You don't need to be going there!

Well, I just might get me a girlfriend

       That's it, idn't it?

Ballads Trees are the mother roots
of all of this work play
ripe with code phrase condensation

face turned toward the wall
means somebody died
probably for love

floating lines show up multiple times
nonce places are not nonsense syllables

*all the
way down*

         *haven of
mineral
here*

                     embodied

on a lee and lonely
bow and balance to me

Ballads / Counter-Ballads

Time rolling language dice
doing things besides just *meaning*
something

the flow of
deep parade

in color
I celebrate

SWEET AUGUST CLEMATIS

Hazy snaky river road where
   white carolina blossoms bloom
            in about three weeks from now

            throwing off on the country air
conditioned world which means the
      windows are all rolled way down

         a vine in heat dries out half brown
                        in front of the church on the
            wrought iron fence we are up

         early these days waiting for
                  the sun to skip its rocks up
                        the river under the bridge

         it hits you like a snake you're
      not willing to hit in the
middle of the blacktop sprawled

      out all the way across the
            winding river road we are
            putting our arms and feet

                  out to catch some air it's so
      hot today like the orange day
            lilies like the orange prison

under the
   mountain

         below the vein
            of the stream   below the
                        rock

suits worn by inmates picking up
trash along the scenic by
ways, a rock outcropping, a

long gun we hope is only
for show held by the man in
back, in black, at least that was

earlier when it wasn't
quite so hot. What bothers me
is something I can't quite pin down

still need
to say

how context
is used

as
mycellium for
mushroom

Connecting
underground
in fiber

AN ELEMENTAL YEAR

for Mary Morgaine

Sometimes I wake with words or a phrase arising from the
dream it seems like the tip of an iceberg or a vine tendril
reach out

to grasp

Yesterday it was

Vital

Vitex

and that was from that day
I first met the tree

also called Chaste Tree

Vitex,

you are Agnus Castra
the castrated lamb

said to be "monk's pepper"
as in saltpeter
so I resist touching you

through
the rock

the way a
river runs

organic

a definative
form   is not simple

thinking,
That's the last thing I need
but one seed jumps into my .
hair

you even out estrogen
your Leaves are opposite

and I wrote *out* of that dream nothing
that
resembled the dream at all

Something stuck with me
Mary said today about
letting whatever I learned
take root & manifest,
stay & grow— the
implication is to — let it settle
& take root in whatever
way it will propagate
itself into a new organic
form
    Vitex
  Vital

Virtually vivant

textually flooding

vital texts she stood
in the middle of the Chaste Tree

of stories

of names   *together*
of facts

She said it is good to let it spread out
Sometimes people trim them too much

they need room

& my daughter said if she had one

she would give it room

   Virtual Vitex

Sweet Vetch says Julie P.
who communicates in these ways

My daughter stood across the circle from me
separates herself from my side
first because of the sun
so connects to me in the circle
of others known and unknown

Often I wake from dream thinking of someone
or many ones

or I get up and write something like

   Bibliomantic

      The mist hasn't burned off the river yet

dance
   the pattern
      the road

      & concrete.
         useful

            at once
               abstract

AILANTHUS

The Tree of Heaven!

   O Garbage Tree!

who grows like gypsies strong even on the edges of dumps
who adapted to Dallas to name their children "J.R."
In back allies of New York City Village
Idiot with rats are rooting around you
in back of 437 East 12th Street where
the neighbors are practicing voodoo
in this mountain field entwined with a pear tree

There must be a reason you are so strong

You are the embodiment of the Tree of Heaven
that Harry Smith drew with all its Secret Alphabets
a greeting card to the Universe

By a stream in Boulder
Harry held up "Horsetail" and told me
"This is an Equestrian Plant"
& I, in turn,
crushed a leaf of you, Ailanthus,
and said to Harry Smith,
this plant smells like Peanut Butter
then he replied
"Ah Yes!
but
What did it smell like
BEFORE
there was
Peanut Butter?"

                         in line time

                                   socio-sensual
                                      affair

AFTER

August's height of heavenly perfume
I never knew what bloomed

after the Sweet August Clematis whose
   myriad white starry flowers turn to green hairy spirals

now I know comes
     the time of the Purple Asters

down the mountainsides like streams

                of Purple Haze
          on all the road banks

     then the time of
Autumn Olive (*Elyagnes umbellata*)
       also known as Silverberry
                or
          Oleaster

      a bright red fruit
      high on lycopene
      with silvery speckled skin

lines up
   conjunct - a

       Context
          means
          Weave
         woven   *a new*
                            weaving

set back
from the road
next to Hearts-a-Burstin's
bright fuchsia and orange
peeled back

verse
furrow
field

& rilke's
persimmon
best
after first frost

as water

*though I
write fast*

WHAT IT'S LIKE UP HERE

Worst kind of essentialisms
coming around the bend
When you think you're perceiving
a "truth" about "the South"
it's just more complicated than that

Take the old Toll Road
The one with old Drovers houses
set apart at the distance
a flock of turkeys could walk in a day —
Heavenly pastoral and specific goat luster

Well this road sees far
and passes such great graves
as one engraved with heaven-bound S.U.V.
swerving off the side of the Holy Mountain

There's this farm right past the graveyard
The mailbox so close it could be another marker
A pond somehow on the *side* of a far off hill
and a swath of sunflowers you would not believe

One day I ambled nearer
with my three year old daughter in tow —

after lying in
my bed

a star staring   or starring

my mind a
stream

we startled to hear rifle reports
rapidly approaching via a man
in barreling golf cart
with ear-protecters
and golden retriever sent forth in search of
the plump bird he had just brought
down

As my eye followed the trajectory of the little
grass path
where his deathcart ran regularly enough to
make a mark
I spied the Sunflowers along its rim
and realized they had been planted as pretty,
golden lures

A No Trespassing / No Hunting sign there
to say "them's my birds not yourn "

Last night a line of fire (forest)
Up the mountain
I didn't see it
Comb its golden way across the distance

like a square

a poem is better

EQUINOCTIAL HONEY SONNET

Hold ceremony in the everyday
Suspend in equinoctial honey

Drink your potion with intention —
a poem can be descriptive medicine

you concoct for yourself
and others in ever-widening spirals

Seen and unseen, couplets
circle into DNA ladders

Eat Something Wild Every Day
and You Will become Wild

Wild on the horizon, circular, the plants
sing their songs of glee all round

So let us sing — equally in night and day to hold
mountains, time, balance deeper into the year

hand
woven   carefully
    because
      slower   the words
           chosen more

TRAIN TIME

Even when Hazel Dickens & Alice Gerard
  sing *who's that*
knocking on my window
    and
   that lonesome graveyard
they sound like a train

  their immediate case
     for collaboration
country & city
    both in me

  This morning was ridiculously gorgeous again
     The dimension of the river in the distance
honking of geese who bring me outside
appear in the middle distance
    over the loops of tracks
       foregrounded
    all in green haze of many shades

  Here nature *does* seem more attached to culture
  more continuous

  Leaves from NC

  Learn this leaf

  Learn it Well

of the time

machine

the slippage of from and form

    admiring a form

We laugh as visitors from the city
    turn their backs to began their descent
once the sun slips down in back of the ridge

Not knowing
Only when the sun is gone
does it flash its inflorescence
on any cloud remaining

Like tonight
    a shape like a puffy orange
        Cat in profile
       chasing five little puffs
      of separate cloud

      on a train
       rapid
     Time lapse shift

      Look Away
look back it's different

     Like with love

how the
    continents drift

      simulated
        to show
           in relation

          together
           & apart

          a different view

but then lions changing

A purple dragon above
then a field
                of

orange cotton balls
in the front
   bigger than the lake
but a similar shape

                Last week was the week of Giant
Dragonflies

The week before   black butterflies
with blue and orange

who now fall from leaves like leaves

overlapping the week of katydids who are still here in the house
deafening and green on top of the frame until executed by the cat

First the panther
then the bear
then the deer   now dead by the road

from each
bald

these mountains
are old   *crack*
                    the c-o-d-e-

                                X

this is
unknown territory

a space where
something could happen

this first week of september
the yellow being hinted at in leaves
singly drops and from a distance
a yellow haze

the wind picks up
as we say

before the mint invades the
    driveway in a good way
crushed by the tires & smells so good
in the heat

Train Time!

We rush to the balcony
  to see
      which way
          it's coming from

the stream of the
      water
            cuts
      the rock soft

            so many
  ridges
      in the distance

                          & around
                              each turn

If she's coming from the west,
we hear her before we see her

    or we see her twice

the river looks like a lake
   so framed

    Headlight, a Dragon's

rails reverb in the valley
a Tibetan bowl of sound

Our family at the banister
Our daughter grows to meet us

exaggerated
  by
imitators

    slightly at the end
       end of the
         line

          a trill in
           the front

             that goes

                up

HEARD TELL

of the time a Civil War soldier was overheard
planning an attack on a Shelton-Laurel farm
out near Allanstand — the man who over-
heard this then decided to warn that farmer.

This man, who was known at the time as
a "slave" slipped out by night to save that
family. It had started to snow. So as not to be
tracked, he walked the whole way across the
cold white mountains — backwards.

for Jerry Plemmons

*when the same
family sings
the
songs*

*for 10
generatons*

*a certain
birdcall
develops*

IF I DON'T SHAKE YOUR HAND
OR HUG YOUR NECK

Just know I want to,
Billy in the low ground

This song has an Extry Part
that I made a little bit crooked

Ain't no sunshine when she's gone

This is a new song
that sounds like an old song.

That's why we like it.

You're every song I ever heard
Sing for me my mockingbird

Usually we start slow and taper off.

Thank you to the folk up in Madison County
for welcoming us in

Two big reasons I can't be Dolly Parton

I'm busted

So Bless your Hearts and other vital organs

context is
lost

GO GET JOSH GOFORTH

Go get Josh Goforth
to tell you that story
(I can't tell it like he does)

about his grandfather
building a moat around his home
So the alligators wouldn't get in

He charges people tolls
to go up Lonesome Mountain Road
Here are some notes

on him and David Holt
I took up at the Democratic
Party Benefit Fish Fry
where I sat next to Pat

Chaw: when he sleeps he leaves it in

Piddling:

Doing something
    you never finish

                    (like this poem!)

when we rely on the
    Cloud

                        the
            pattern like

a table
    of coverlet
elements

Tree house =
  2 boards

Jimmy Rogers' Last Meal

I heard the
  warden say

Son you
  have one
    more day

Hearing things like

He buttered his bread, now he can lay in it
She had a southern explosion

I've decided to become a veterinarian —
I'm not a natural born carnival.

Them girls were wearing their zucchinis

Sorry for the smell in the house
  I cleaned it with pneumonia

  link to
the person who
    listens

          & sings back

                    Community
                its trans species

          knee to knee
              with the tree

                    complex still
                        needs facts

Reminds me of my mom saying
the Sprint store was the Sprite
store and her knowing I was going
to put that in a poem somewhere

Everybody's got someone like that
in their family and I cultivate it

Ms. Malaprop
She's not solid gone
She's my Mom

If you're not raising your hand you
probably *are* them

of Time   the River

turn &
find a form   the dreams

each night

1000s upon
1000s of

animal
dreams

SARVIS

I've seen the Sarvis bloom
diaphanous white from far off

while the mountainside
is still brown
It's almost Japanese

though I've yet to see
white on white
blooms over snow

A kind of canny lullaby
A historic caution

Sarvis is the way the old folks say
Service — as in when the

circuit rider preacher
came through after ice thaw
to conduct weddings, baptisms
and funerals

that he couldn't reach sooner
before the first breath of spring
alighted

When Uncle Dudley was a boy
brightly he brought his mother a branch

connected
multiplicities

the story of
each plant in its
grand

flowering white
and because she had showed him
an earlier flower which she named
The First Breath of Spring

He said, Look! Mama!
Here is
The *Second* breath of Spring

shining
    diversities
        of these   human made
                            patterns

                    to complex
                        biodome

                                    somehow
                                        simplify

DECORATION DAY

Graves bloom on gray hills
Bright reds, yellows, orange
Chrysanthemums

Christ's anthems
Intentionally bright
So they can be seen

From a long way off
Skyway drive December
Payments in the slot below

decorate the day
Today I remember
Let no mortal flesh

Keep silent til the last
Trumpet calls as they say
It's Decoration Day

Even purple as royal
and various as mushrooms
that dot the woods

the double bow knot   in design

                              like _____

                                    ___ ___

          I want to write

                              the tip of the
                        iceberg

In August this month's
Opposite — Diadems of
Nature's hand call out

We are here we are here
Beneath the ground
And in the very air

Jumping to Jerusalem
Just like John
The lichen of Reminders

That I'm gonna be ready
I'm gonna be ready
I'm gonna be ready

Walking to Jerusalem
Just like John
Say Darling Say

What are those
File cabinets up on the hill?

Bee boxes with rocks on top
Snow dusted mountains
Like dinosaurs head down

the difference
        between
a coverlet
        a quilt

thread text a coverlet constantly weaves

In the Kingdom of Madison
people visit underground
families all year long

hilltop cemetery
dinner-on-the grounds
picnic with the ancestors
and asking of each one

what will my portion be
last summer I rounded
the bend on the Ivy River
one Sunday afternoon

three church's worth
of folks holding baptism
in the stream —
the same road where

a rainbow arced over
the spring before
I have a picture
to prove it though

so glad to see it
in person these
churches what were
the community

collage

a quilt

is being pieced together from
cut materials sewn

a coverlet is
woven anew

context equals
coverl[

stronghold still hold
and sing— one is called
Freedom, one Little
Flower and they
dot the hills all over

ballad ornamentation
sliding up into a note
rather than stepping on it

ridgetop to ridgetop
it's about commitment
to memory

Cumi at the base
of our mountain
John and now Louise

I decorate their Days
in this book of praise

google it I
   mean   thread
                means
         the word
           means
          context   I'm trying not
                       to drop the
                       thread

SHAPE NOTE

sung in a square
fa like a little flag
sol round like the sun
the rest I just sing

sing a medieval minor
musical layer-cake
akin to the celtic
call and response

and am I born to die
to lay this body down
And must my trembling spirit rise
Into a world unknown

solid in a square
someday I will go
to the center and lead
but for now I sing my part

play party shoe around
let's have a candy pulling now
of sweet evocation of when
the hills were draped with song

the thread
of the bed

we read about
how you cant
google context
& so she
does — google
context I mean
crossways
the pull of

EXPLODING PUSSYWILLOWS OF
EARLY EARLY SPRING

What happens next?
     as she points
        to a green
            leaf
       bursting
    from
    a grey brown
      stick

Forced they are
     but it works
(inside the table again)

how they
  evolve differently in
    each valley here

              not being
          able to
        get over the
          dry
            ridge

   asks the child   so now to cook and write

      Is 10 minutes
         up yet

                    I'm
                  really
               hungry
              are you?

Pollen memory possum car
Lights at the crossroads
Everything has eyes
Little Pine Nite Hunt
Down by the river alone — together

Yea, though I walk through the
Valley of the Shadow of Self
I shall fear no People
My River family comforteth me
As do the ones on the Ridge

Time and the River are on my side
As four divides into five

Branch of spring
 Pollinated next to
        Dandelion
        Explosion

specificity
    lives in moisture
              every rock &
                riff pushed
                 forms a new
                    interrelated

                  quote biodiversity
              of song

              salamander
                & mushroom

                  the facts about
                  the divergent

STILL SHINE

This ain't your average, everyday hot-buttered popcorn, Sutton
The fine art of moonshine isn't hard to master, Panther Breath

Faster, Cat Daddy, faster
If you're willing to Popskull past the butter road
to where Tiger's Sweat meets the moonshine blanched land

You'll see Sweet Spirits of Cats A-fighting!
Alchemically join Happy Sally and
Blue John round the bend, then
Jump Steady with Block and Tackle
to See Seven Stars!

Eye of Rotgut
Toe of Mulekick
Bubble bubble
Ruckus juice

far in the future
& the past

adjunct to Africa
at one point

down the coast
and inland

to the Appalachian
frame

then jump over

to join
England - Scotland
again

Fizzing gizzards galore, Batcave man!
Let's publish this in the *Chanticlear Batcave Gazette!*

Brown mountain lights Shine Shine shine

A double-tanked hopped-up hoopty
Barrels down Thunder Road
One tank full of gas
the other carrying something quicker
a.k.a the Oil of Gladness

Let us be true to Cool Water, Old Horsey
Raise a Masonic Jar
clear full of
One another

Sometimes you just have to let loooose

the dance is a
      turning geometry

            a thread backwards
            & forwards to
      the context of

                  the river's
            serpentine pulls   which is
                              under our
                                    feet
                                       the old
                                          country

AT FIRST BLUE

> Awaked by the train
> through the snow
> All the poets
> Come to visit
> one by one
> from the shelves

David Henderson's
> hot *Neo-California* /
in the nation of Aztlan
> works up a
> rhythm in the silence
> of the monitor lizard heater
Eric calls his
"Girlfriend 500"

Blood comes
> with new
> snow
> wakes me up in time
for first blue
> now purple

weave
> *their water*
> *fingers*

> *coverlets*
> *of water*

> *turns into a Quilt*

> *hallucinatory*
> *Square dance*

> *the music*
> *turns likewise*

> *(under the*
> *Moon)*

On the porch
  in purple sheet
flannel
  the moon
already half
way down from
  full blue on
the eve of
  New Year
      New Decade
the train's eye
  the light
    calls
  to what

empty & full
  local knowledge
  that extends
a jumping point

To clear the trees
from the roads
  they work like dogs
Sea glass in a bottle
in the Leaf Room
  Under down
      generating dreaming
Our mothers sleep

serpentine
worn down

the river
running over
    green

      thirst & turn   so

        what else
makes the passages

        cross
woven the
    context

too I hope
 soundly in their
 beds
Owls still live
 behind the house
 looking down from
  oaks

My daughter's
 first poem

is written (drawn) "in Japanese"

and translates as

Sun Sun Sun
 Come out to play

Sun Sun Sun
 Come out

Her first poem consciously
 called that —
There have been others
 Recorded and noted

I record them not to take them
  but to praise and keep them safe —
 They are hers!

but

                    how do you
                      know it's
                       the earth's
                       3rd Oldest
                        River

She has also made
a hummingbird
   of wire & tissue
paper perched on
   a branch
sipping from a
   huge red flower

with aid from
   others —
we help to bend
   the wire & secure
the branch
 in the wood

  at her direction
she forms the
 bird of color
I scribble in purple
 crayon
 The sky lightens
my return to
 bed?
The snow is
 blue, black trees
& deck, mist
 clouds
The earth is
 turning & painted
on her desk
 the red part is actually lava pools

it
wrinkled up   worn
      down

        The rocks below

Frost Flowers &
the snow on
   distant mountain and
a million acres
      of sky!

Pink, pink boots
  to the stratosphere

  Sunrise in outer space
  love for everybody

We need it
here on Planet Earth

Shinbone Rock,
    Humpback Mountain, Pretty Hollow

EQUINOX HYMN

All hail the power of Equinox
Earth, Water, Air and Fire

The Noon Sun beams his blessings down
To wed him we aspire

The Full Moon beams her blessings down
To wed her we aspire

All rocks   All trees All waterfalls
All passionflowers in light

Bring forth your flowery diadems
To crown us Day and Night

Bring forth your flowery diadems
And crown us Day and Night

All hail the power of Equinox
Now Day and Night are one

The orbits of all heavenly spheres
All planets Stars and Sun

The orbits of all heavenly spheres
are balanced now as One

Tahkeyostee meaning 'where they race'

POKE SALLET

is cooked not raw

> *stay ahead*
> *of the red*

Eat in spring
   cook when 6 inches or less

lymph cleanser

  2 boils

Do Not drink the potlikker

Eat the berry

1 on the 1st day
2 on the 2nd day
3 on the 3rd

How far do you do
spit out the poisonous seeds?

become a dynamic accumulator
bringing up minerals from below

the rapids below Asheville

        to the French Broad
specifically they gave the name Agiqua,

Children in a school near here used poke ink
It was that with which they wrote

my daughter paints her arms

the way to play the plants

on paper the unfixed juice goes from bright magen-
ta to a dried blood color

the man who built our house
first dreamed of a pokeberry sky

but after a hot day of crushing berries
and smearing the boards, gave into Benjamin Moore

it's "hard to fix"

that color more bright than cochineal

to fit its moods and natures.

this river needed several names

HOW TO PRONOUNCE APPALACHIA
OR *OVERSHOT DICTIONARY OF WOVEN NAMES*
DRAWN FROM OUT THE BLACK BOX OF HISTORY

for Francis Louisa Goodrich great-granddaughter of Noah Webster who
drew up the coverlet designs of Western Carolina thus encouraging their
continuance

for Selinde Lanier whose coverlet weaving studio is named String Theory

for Betty Smith who wove Bettie Sellers' "Incantation for a New Coat" on
her Psaltry

If life were as long as art, I might come nearer to the goal of comple-
tion, but no dictionary or encyclopedia holds the knowledge I seek
ELIZA CALVERT HALL

You have to be spare, pull back, abstract
Think of the page as a field
"some of the places I knew names of"

Don't pretend there is one big continuous well thought out truth
BRENDA COULTAS

The Cherokee were right.

subhorizontal crystalline thrust sheets

miles buried beneath

I don't want to be no cultural stripminer

I'm just scratching the surface here

pointing the way

   for you to take your own foray

your own *I do this I do that* walk-up

to Meadow Fork   or   Metaphor

bypass the Mondo Tire Rim Cloud Chamber Bowl Gamelan
suspended

pass Riddle Farm Road

pass Mother's Way

pass O. Henry's house floating around on risers

pass the ghost of the drive-in movie theater now a tobacco field

over the folded and faulted margin

thrust belt province

the blue ridge

pass the bypass Inventor's Mailbox on a String

    whose very long white rope
    doubles back from road to porch
    so the mailbox can be
    pulleyed back and forth
    and this inventor doesn't even have to leave
    the porch to get the mail

find again the Slingshot Man

who handed me a hand-carved slingshot wrapped round
with a Bible verse because King David used them too

past the things they carried and then let go

to "hit the seam" at the bottom of the frame

with a name that sounds oftentimes like a song or a poem

find an altar made of coal the next state over
draw your map of Appalachia — eveyone's is different

        igneous and metamorphic rocks

          the crystalline Appalachians

            collectively known as

Here are the names celestial:

Hickory Leaf
McElroy
Pine Bloom
Rose in the Wilderness
King's Flower
Cat Track

Sunrise   (more?)

There are as many names of coverlets as women who wove them

threading   is similar to music

mathematical

making the cloth
from the ground swell up

 not just pasting it on the surface

or piecework

blue ridge, piedmant, adirondack

and new england provinces

ocean that
was Ohio

and what about what Eliza Calvert Hall wrote as she wrote on the
ontology of the coverlet in 1937:

*I pass a negro cabin and on the clothes-line or the fence hangs a bed-cover
inherited from "Old Mistress," spun and woven, probably, on the old
plantation in slave days by the skilled fingers of "black Mammy."*

I think who owns the loom thought they got to claim the coverlet
but the fingers that labor own the pattern once they weave it

Who make it owns it

a self-made woman owns herself
and all her own late night forms

in 2007 Brenda Coultas wrote:

I wonder Are there any abolitionists hanging from our family tree

and Sappho:

>   *O mother*
>   *I cannot work the loom*

raised up
    beside the
Pre Cambrian

        continental
         shelf

            underneath it all

I am sick with love for the poem

In pulling the threads out what is lost

sometimes to unravel is a good thing
but learn to interweave

variations on an old pattern
but don't lose track
of the old one
so you can come back to its lovely form
for another variation

Leave enough mushrooms for the next crop to grow back
Dump the spores in the yard after washing the wild chantarelles

The South is my toponomastic heaven

All our reality is named in language.
All place names are made up place names.
All theories are wrong and some are useful.
but O   the ecstasy of naming

there is this river

how do you know

*everyone always
asks*

the confusion of Apple names

Cat Head etc

Yellow Transparent
Wilson's Red June
Red Cheese "a good keeper"

I have found Eden and you are my Eve
said Rip to Ruth

Apples do not grow above "the Northern limit belt"

Definition of SUBURBIA: The place where they tear down
the trees then names the streets after them.

I think of Eve and remember how to

"throw an Apple at cha"

through it all an Ode.
a love song
  The river is the song
      that goes on   on

              renew   renew

        mountains call to you

even

"though some girls scutched well"

Does one learn the pattern better if one knows the latinate name
or if one eats the mushrooms for dinner with peaches and rice?

If one saves a moth from the sink to let it go on the porch?

who cried out

    and I was not moved?

A coverlet was taken apart to wash or mend
and often sewn back together   again

in a different way to help distribute wear

kind of like rotating tires

Problems with apple names arose

alternation   *endless spark of*
repetition   *variation*

      older than heart
        switch back leads
      thriving over a new leaf soil

In the first place

southern rural families

were isolated

By both distance and poor roads.

Apple trees were acquired
from neighbors or tree peddlers
Renamed, using the new owner's name,

When slaves gained their freedom,
some shed their erstwhile names
and took on "Person" or "Freeman"

or a garbled version of the original name,
or a characteristic of the apple
such as color,
size,
or time of ripening.   The archive of apples reworked

in the wrinkles of
serpentine   of limestone   of
rivers pushed into moisture
older than the hills

The ice age packed   all the seeds
of the CONTINENTAL DRIFT
down
to this sheer place & they thrived

As the frontier moved westward,
Other confusion was also at work.

Tree peddlers, faced with a request for a specific apple variety
were not above relabeling a tree to avoid losing a sale.

Now there's this lust for vintage authenticity
Globalization of apple, loss of apple specificity

Pomological Diagram from which a serial poem could be
cultivated:

Roundish Oblong Oblate Conical or Ribbed
Genealogies of apple vs. The Awful Red Delicious

To learn what is still unknown to me about names,

drafts and designs

I would have to make a pilgrimage . . .

stopping at every doorway

green variety
into red
berries its salamander its lichen way

and asking an alms
of information with such questions as these:

After you dip your magnets in—What else is in the box
(Historical thinking)

Are "Flourishing Wave" and "Floating Wave" the same as
"Ocean Wave"?

Can you hear the synaptic frying
When you say history is not the past?

What are the differences between
"Iron Wheel"
"Running Wheel"
"Wheel of Fortune"   ·
"Wheel of Time" and
     pilot wheel?

O I wonder what's still in the box
More in there than not

What flower is King's Flower intended to represent?

Was Lee's Surrender named in sorrow or in triumph?

a holler
whose crotch of color

brewed in
millenia of dampness
between every ridge a valley

Difference is what makes meaning happen

"I will let the apples speak for themselves."

A laying on of names and a renaming

Mrs. Davis gave Frances Goodrich a Double Bowknot:

AKA

Hickory Leaf,
Muscadine Hulls,
or Double Muscadine Hulls.

saying "I've brought you a present,
knowing that you take delight in such as this."

Francis drew out its organic grid on a graph

as receipt for future forms

to weave on

and then she, the great granddaughter of Noah Webster

to another stash
of living things, a new
permutation

a panoply of walks
in every ridge a bridge

set to drawing the next pattern out
got the ladies to "put out"

and half convinced Sodom to become Revere
a more New England-y name
        not getting the humor therein contained

and as she read the thread

    Eliza scribed
...*The colonial coverlet is to American art what the prose
works of Increase Mather and the verses of Anne Bradstreet
are to American literature.*

Can you read these
Double Chariot Wheels?

these double muscadine hulls

        the fact about the no plantations
        in the mountains doesn't mean
        there were no slaves

        In Dante (rhyme it with can't)
        it was said to me that

everybody's the same color as the mine

                who will take care of it

                        *No one owns the river
                        Same with language*

takes me to Affrilachia
and Frank X. Walker's
aptly named "Blues Ridge"

no mills, no mines

no mortgage here

places named Sodom
wanted no part in the war

the Kingdom of Madison

a salty sovereignty

weave into cloth

some sacred geometry

the green serpentine

line of stone which joins us up

to use the patterns, as gatha graph

Cat tracks   and Snail Trail

*Instead of feeding the cat
or waking the child   well I do feed
the familiar*

Pine Tree and Jack

Because of alignment

"The boss's brains are under the worker's cap."

the tobacco girls

(a pack of 'em)
threw it all on the table

in the pines

if you are able

toward the wall

threw off her clothes

she threw them on the table

A Table is a repeating grid

*I write this poem
almost in one go*

not really

under a February full moon

Not as the dog walks
but as the crow flies
over complexities' roads

face turned toward the

back of this photograph is marked:

"Seven stars. Wrong side out."

Yellow made from peach leaves.

"Seven Stars. Woven"

led her to collect weaving patterns
much in the same way that others
of that era were collecting mountain songs

Broom, Broom
Sweep the Room
Break the warp of yesterday

the water is always moving

from an Appalachian Spring

"Lasting Beauty" is unknown

    Broom, Broom
    Clean the corner
    Make a Place for My New Love

radiates out eventually forming interlocking wheels

    Robin, Robin
    Twirl the Bobbin
    Whirl the Bobbin
    Sing, Sing
    Robin, Robin
    Fill the Bobbin
    Turn the Black Sheep's wool to gold

shot through with

Riddle, Riddle
Throw the Shuttle
Warm the wall with April Sun

What tunes can you play into my tape recorder that will be lost forever

        You've got problems if you insist on boundaries

the gift that started Allanstand

Room, Room
Scent of Violets
For the Neck
of his new coat

Linger, Linger
On My Finger
Little ring so shiny bright

and, when all other ways failed, taking the "footpath way."

Linger, Linger
Oh My Love
in this coat of
Black Sheep's Wool

The ghost of festivals past
Same with language

Water is a living thing
Water is a moving thing

COVERLET

I'm glad for worship houses
People build around the world

But the *garden* is my church
The woods, my sanctuary

To do a little dance
On a screened-in porch

While no one is looking
In my own dimension

Find each her own motif
A shady place

Ants filter in timed array

A start & stop

Coverlet

"Let us not be poetic but practical."

"*Because the river belongs to everyone it belongs to no one.*"

for Wilma Dykeman

RIVER CODEX

NOTES ON POEMS

"A Letter Out" began as a letter to Linda Kozloff-
Turner; some poems in "Fieldwork" were written during
the "Living Well Inside and Out" workshop taught by
Mary Morgaine in the Fall of 2010. The saying in italics
in "Equinoctial Honey Sonnet" is by naturalist Frank
Cook; "Equinox Hymn"refigures the hymn "All Hail the
Power of Jesus' Name" and can be sung to the tune of
CORONATION by Oliver Holden, 1793; "Little Black
Boxes" and "Sheila Kay on the Child Ballads" were written
from notes taken during a concert by the great ballad
singer Sheila Kay Adams in Asheville, NC; "To Raise an
A" was written from notes from a workshop with master
stone carver Phinias Chirubvu at Camille Shaffer's artists'
retreat project, Azule; "Dulcimer" takes its shape from
a dulcimer made by Clifford Glenn and uses text from
Appendix D of *The Story of the Dulcimer* by Ralph Lee
Smith; "Mushroom Walker" is for Peggy Ahwesh and
Ken Crouse who took me on my first mushroom forays;
"If I Don't Shake Your Hand or Hug Your Neck" features
commentary between songs at the 2013 New Year's Eve
Concert by Josh Goforth, Laura Boosinger, Ralph Lewis
and Sons of Ralph at the Madison County Arts Council,
Marshall, NC; "Go Get Josh Goforth" contains notes
taken during a Democratic Party Benefit Concert by Josh
Goforth and David Holt at Madison County High School;
"Shape Note" contains a stanza from *Idumea* (Sacred Harp),
words by Charles Wesley; music by Ananias Davisson;
"Exploding Pussywillows of Early Early Spring" is for Erin
O'Neal upon the birth of her daughter PINATOVA LEE
O'Neal, March 8th, 2007; "Still Shine" quotes nicknames
for moonshine on display at the Mountain Heritage Center
at Western Carolina University, Cullowhee, NC;

"How to Pronounce Appalachia OR Overshot Dictionary of Woven Names Drawn from out the Black Box of History" uses quotations and allusions to many texts including: *Mountain Homespun* by Francis Louisa Goodrich; *A Book of Hand-Woven Coverlets*, by Eliza Calvert Hall; *Handicrafts of the Southern Highlands with an Account of the Rural Handicraft Movement of the United States and Suggestions for the Wider Use of Handicrafts in Adult Education and Recreation* by Allen H. Eaton, Containing Fifty-eight Illustrations from Photographs Taken for the Work by Doris Ulmann; Frank X. Walker's *Affrilacia* and *Black Box—Poems by Frank X. Walker* (Old Cove Press); "Old Southern Apples" by Creighton Lee Calhoun, Jr., Blue Ridge Archive, Ferrum College, Ferrum, VA; "Incantation for a New Coat" words by poet, Bettie Sellers, music by Betty Smith on her album, *Both Sides: Then & Now* (Bluff Mountain Music);

"Coverlet" contains a quote engraved on a stone at the John C. Campbell Folk School in Brasstown, NC;

"RIVER CODEX" contains fragments and lines from *The French Broad* by Wilma Dykeman to whom the poem is dedicated. Dykeman wrote a total of eighteen books, both nonfiction and fiction. *The French Broad* was her first and was published in 1955 as part of the famous Holt Rhinehart Rivers of America Series; additionally, the poem includes Jamie Townsend's "dollywood" line.

Throughout, italicized lines are either quotes, overheard, or should be sung. RIVER CODEX is designed to be read either forwards or backwards, stanza by stanza, throughout the book.

c

ACKNOWLEDGEMENTS

Thank you to the Editors of the following publications, in which versions of these poems have appeared:

The Asheville Poetry Review, editor, Keith Flynn; *The Cambridge Literary Review*, "Cross-Genre Women" guest editor, Emily Critchley, general editor, Boris Jardine; *Dome Poem*, video by Tony Torn, Lee Ann Brown and David Fuhrer; *Far From the Centers of Ambition*, editors Rand Brandes and Lee Ann Brown, (Lenoir-Rhyne University/ Lorimer Press); *Kindergarde: Avant-garde Poems, Plays, Stories, and Songs for Children*, A Small Press Traffic project published by Black Radish Books, editor, Dana Teen Lomax; *mem*, guest editor: Laynie Brown, series editor, Jill Stengel; *Root Stock: A Farm Friends Publication*, edited by Miekel And; *Van Gogh's Ear: Poetry for the New Millenium*, editor Dawn Michelle-Baude, Paris, France; *Wordplay*, a weekly poetry radio show, hosted by Jeff Davis's Asheville, NC; *Wildflowers: A Woodstock mountain poetry anthology*, editor, Shiv Mirabito.

Some poems evolved during these residencies, projects and fellowships: The Howard Foundation Fellowship, 2005-2006; Regional Studies: An Appalachian Exemplar, National Endowment for the Humanities Summer Institute, Ferrum College, Ferrum, VA, July 2006; Sabbatical from St. John's University, Fall 2010.

d

THANK YOU to **Harry Smith** who led me to **Bascom Lamar Lunsford** who said things like: *The banjo brings out the balladry in my system, whereupon, I began the erection of a musical layer-cake, with work and school as a filling, and such social ingredients as bean stringin's, butter stirrin's, apple peelin's, Shoe-arounds, Candy breakins, Log rollins . . .*

. . . who led me to Madison County where things like this can still happen, which led me to Sunnybank and **Elmer Hall** who led me to **Betty Smith**, weaver of words, threads and musical notes who led me to many others especially **Jane Gentry** who sang all day long no matter what she was doing and to **Wilma Dykeman** whose beloved French Broad River I write from right to left flowing southeast to northwest throughout this book, and to **Francis Louisa Goodrich** who led me to "an unknown source." Big Love to all whose words spiral throughout this book, especially to my daughter **Miranda Lee Reality Torn**, and to my great encourager and loving husband, **Tony Torn**. Thank you to everyone in Madison County who says "Welcome Home" each time we return.

FENCE BOOKS

OTTOLINE PRIZE

Inter Arma	Lauren Shufran

MOTHERWELL & ALBERTA PRIZE

Negro League Baseball	Harmony Holiday
living must bury	Josie Sigler
Aim Straight at the Fountain and Press Vaporize	Elizabeth Marie Young
Unspoiled Air	Kaisa Ullsvik Miller
The Cow	Ariana Reines
Practice, Restraint	Laura Sims
A Magic Book	Sasha Steensen
Sky Girl	Rosemary Griggs
The Real Moon of Poetry and Other Poems	Tina Brown Celona
Zirconia	Chelsey Minnis

FENCE MODERN POETS SERIES

In the Laurels, Caught	Lee Ann Brown
Eyelid Lick	Donald Dunbar
Nick Demske	Nick Demske
Duties of an English Foreign Secretary	Macgregor Card
Star in the Eye	James Shea
Structure of the Embryonic Rat Brain	Christopher Janke
The Stupefying Flashbulbs	Daniel Brenner
Povel	Geraldine Kim
The Opening Question	Prageeta Sharma
Apprehend	Elizabeth Robinson
The Red Bird	Joyelle McSweeney

NATIONAL POETRY SERIES

Your Invitation to a Modest Breakfast	Hannah Gamble
A Map Predetermined and Chance	Laura Wetherington
The Network	Jena Osman
The Black Automaton	Douglas Kearney
Collapsible Poetics Theater	Rodrigo Toscano

ANTHOLOGIES & CRITICAL WORKS

Not for Mothers Only: Contemporary Poets on Child-Getting & Child-Rearing
Catherine Wagner & Rebecca Wolff, editors
A Best of Fence: *The First Nine Years*, Volumes 1 & 2
Rebecca Wolff and Fence Editors, editors

POETRY

A Book Beginning What and Ending Away	Clark Coolidge
88 Sonnets	Clark Coolidge
Mellow Actions	Brandon Downing
Percussion Grenade	Joyelle McSweeney
Coeur de Lion	Ariana Reines
June	Daniel Brenner
English Fragments A Brief History of the Soul	Martin Corless-Smith
The Sore Throat & Other Poems	Aaron Kunin
Dead Ahead	Ben Doller
My New Job	Catherine Wagner
Stranger	Laura Sims
The Method	Sasha Steensen
The Orphan & Its Relations	Elizabeth Robinson
Site Acquisition	Brian Young
Rogue Hemlocks	Carl Martin
19 Names for Our Band	Jibade-Khalil Huffman
Infamous Landscapes	Prageeta Sharma
Bad Bad	Chelsey Minnis
Snip Snip!	Tina Brown Celona
Yes, Master	Michael Earl Craig
Swallows	Martin Corless-Smith
Folding Ruler Star	Aaron Kunin
The Commandrine & Other Poems	Joyelle McSweeney
Macular Hole	Catherine Wagner
Nota	Martin Corless-Smith
Father of Noise	Anthony McCann
Can You Relax in My House	Michael Earl Craig
Miss America	Catherine Wagner

FICTION

Prayer and Parable: Stories	Paul Maliszewski
Flet: A Novel	Joyelle McSweeney
The Mandarin	Aaron Kunin